CHILDHOOD FEARS AND ANXIETIES

CATASTROPHES

CHILDHOOD FEARS AND ANXIETIES

Anxiety and Fear in Daily Life

Catastrophes

Crime and Terrorism

Family Fears

Medical Fears

Nighttime Fears

Phobias

School Fears

Separation Anxiety

Social Fears

Symptoms and Treatments of Anxiety Disorders

CHILDHOOD FEARS
AND ANXIETIES

CATASTROPHES

H.W. POOLE

SERIES CONSULTANT
ANNE S. WALTERS, Ph.D.

Emma Pendleton Bradley Hospital

Warren Alpert Medical School of
Brown University

Mason Crest
450 Parkway Drive, Suite D
Broomall, PA 19008
www.masoncrest.com

© 2018 by Mason Crest, an imprint of National Highlights, Inc. All rights reserved. No part of this publication may be reproduced or transmitted in any form or by any means, electronic or mechanical, including photocopying, recording, taping, or any information storage and retrieval system, without permission from the publisher.

MTM Publishing, Inc.
435 West 23rd Street, #8C
New York, NY 10011
www.mtmpublishing.com

President: Valerie Tomaselli
Vice President, Book Development: Hilary Poole
Designer: Annemarie Redmond
Copyeditor: Peter Jaskowiak
Editorial Assistant: Leigh Eron

Series ISBN: 978-1-4222-3721-2
Hardback ISBN: 978-1-4222-3723-6
E-Book ISBN: 978-1-4222-8056-0

Library of Congress Cataloging-in-Publication Data
Names: Poole, Hilary W., author.
Title: Catastrophes / by H.W. Poole; series consultant: Anne S. Walters, Ph.D., Emma Pendleton Bradley Hospital, Alpert Medical School/Brown University.
Description: Broomall, PA: Mason Crest, [2018] | Series: Childhood fears and anxieties | Audience: Age: 12+ | Audience: Grade 7 to 8. | Includes index.
Identifiers: LCCN 2017007427 (print) | LCCN 2017023797 (ebook) | ISBN 9781422280560 (ebook) | ISBN 9781422237212 (series ISBN) | ISBN 9781422237236 (hardback: alk. paper)
Subjects: LCSH: Disasters—Psychological aspects—Juvenile literature. | Anxiety—Juvenile literature.
Classification: LCC BF789.D5 (ebook) | LCC BF789.D5 P66 2017 (print) | DDC 155.9/35—dc23
LC record available at https://lccn.loc.gov/2017007427

Printed and bound in the United States of America.

First printing
9 8 7 6 5 4 3 2 1

QR CODES AND LINKS TO THIRD PARTY CONTENT
You may gain access to certain third party content ("Third Party Sites") by scanning and using the QR Codes that appear in this publication (the "QR Codes"). We do not operate or control in any respect any information, products or services on such Third Party Sites linked to by us via the QR Codes included in this publication and we assume no responsibility for any materials you may access using the QR Codes. Your use of the QR Codes may be subject to terms, limitations, or restrictions set forth in the applicable terms of use or otherwise established by the owners of the Third Party Sites. Our linking to such Third Party Sites via the QR Codes does not imply an endorsement or sponsorship of such Third Party Sites, or the information, products or services offered on or through the Third Party Sites, nor does it imply an endorsement or sponsorship of this publication by the owners of such Third Party Sites.

TABLE OF CONTENTS

Series Introduction 6
Chapter One: Scary World 9
Chapter Two: Living with Uncertainty 17
Chapter Three: Preparation 25
Chapter Four: Recovery 35
Further Reading 44
Series Glossary 45
Index 47
About the Advisor 48
About the Author 48
Photo Credits 48

Key Icons to Look for:

Words to Understand: These words with their easy-to-understand definitions will increase the reader's understanding of the text, while building vocabulary skills.

Sidebars: This boxed material within the main text allows readers to build knowledge, gain insights, explore possibilities, and broaden their perspectives by weaving together additional information to provide realistic and holistic perspectives.

Educational Videos: Readers can view videos by scanning our QR codes, which will provide them with additional educational content to supplement the text. Examples include news coverage, moments in history, speeches, iconic sports moments, and much more.

Text-Dependent Questions: These questions send the reader back to the text for more careful attention to the evidence presented there.

Research Projects: Readers are pointed toward areas of further inquiry connected to each chapter. Suggestions are provided for projects that encourage deeper research and analysis.

Series Glossary of Key Terms: This back-of-the-book glossary contains terminology used throughout the series. Words found here increase the reader's ability to read and comprehend higher-level books and articles in this field.

SERIES INTRODUCTION

Who among us does not have memories of an intense childhood fear? Fears and anxieties are a part of *every* childhood. Indeed, these fears are fodder for urban legends and campfire tales alike. And while the details of these legends and tales change over time, they generally have at their base predictable childhood terrors such as darkness, separation from caretakers, or bodily injury.

We know that fear has an evolutionary component. Infants are helpless, and, compared to other mammals, humans have a very long developmental period. Fear ensures that curious children will stay close to caretakers, making them less likely to be exposed to danger. This means that childhood fears are adaptive, making us more likely to survive, and even thrive, as a species.

Unfortunately, there comes a point when fear and anxiety cease to be useful. This is especially problematic today, for there has been a startling increase in anxiety among children and adolescents. In fact, 25 percent of 13- to 18-year-olds now have mild to moderate anxiety, and the *median* age of onset for anxiety disorders is just 11 years old.

Why might this be? Some say that the contemporary United States is a nation preoccupied with risk, and it is certainly possible that our children are absorbing this preoccupation as well. Certainly, our exposure to potential threats has never been greater. We see graphic images via the media and have more immediate news of all forms of disaster. This can lead our children to feel more vulnerable, and it may increase the likelihood that they respond with fear. If children based their fear on the news that they see on Facebook or on TV, they would dramatically overestimate the likelihood of terrible things happening.

As parents or teachers, what do we do about fear? As in other areas of life, we provide our children with guidance and education on a daily basis. We teach them about the signs and feelings of fear. We discuss and normalize typical fear reactions, and support them in tackling difficult situations despite fear. We explain—and demonstrate by example—how to identify "negative thinking traps" and generate positive coping thoughts instead.

But to do so effectively, we might need to challenge some of our own assumptions about fear. Adults often assume that they must protect their children from fear and help them to avoid scary situations, when sometimes the best course is for the child to face the fear and conquer it. This is counterintuitive for many adults: after all, isn't it our job to reassure our children and help them feel better? Yes, of course! Except when it isn't. Sometimes they need us to help them confront their fears and move forward anyway.

That's where these volumes come in. When it comes to fear, balanced information is critical. Learning about fear as it relates to many different areas can help us to help our children remember that although you don't choose whether to be afraid, you do choose how to handle it. These volumes explore the world of childhood fears, seeking to answer important questions: How much is too much? And how can fear be positive, functioning to mobilize us in the face of danger?

Fear gives us the opportunity to step up and respond with courage and resilience. It pushes us to expand our sphere of functioning to areas that might feel unfamiliar or risky. When we are a little nervous or afraid, we tend to prepare a little more, look for more information, ask more questions—and all of this can function to help us expand the boundaries of our lives in a positive direction. So, while fear might *feel* unpleasant, there is no doubt that it can have a positive outcome.

Let's teach our children that.

—Anne Walters, Ph.D.
Chief Psychologist, Emma Pendleton Bradley Hospital
Clinical Associate Professor,
Alpert Medical School of Brown University

CHAPTER ONE

SCARY WORLD

Your parents and grandparents grew up in a period of history called the Cold War, an era of tension between the United States and the Soviet Union (now Russia). The war was "cold" because the two countries did not fight each other directly. But people were afraid that the two powers *might* go to war against each other, possibly with nuclear weapons. To prepare, schools held "duck and cover" drills, where students learned to hide under their desks in hopes of surviving a nuclear bomb. Back then, a nuclear war was by far the scariest catastrophe people could imagine.

These days, the prospect of a nuclear conflict with Russia seems remote. We are actually much safer today than in the past—and not just from nuclear war. For example, crime rates are down, and diseases like smallpox and polio are no longer a problem. But students today practice another type of drill, sometimes called "lockdown," to prepare for the possibility of a school shooting. Meanwhile, the potential for a large-scale terror attack is never far from our minds. And scientists tell us that natural

WORDS TO UNDERSTAND

anthropogenic: caused by human action.

berate: to criticize harshly.

drought: an extended period with no rain.

evacuate: to leave a dangerous place and go to a safer one.

disasters like hurricanes and earthquakes will happen more often as the Earth continues to warm. Sometimes it may feel like potential catastrophes lurk behind every corner.

WHAT ARE CATASTROPHES?

We throw around the word *catastrophe* a lot—in casual conversation, it's just a quick way to describe a big mess. For example, your parents might describe your bedroom as a "catastrophe" right before they make you clean it. But the word does actually have a concrete definition: a catastrophe is an event that causes major problems and suffering among a group of people. The group could be large or small. For instance, a hurricane is a type of catastrophe that affects an entire region, while your house burning down is a catastrophe that only affects your family. Strictly defined, a catastrophe isn't something that only happens to you—it happens to a group of which you're a member.

We usually divide catastrophes (also called disasters) into two categories: natural and **anthropogenic** (human-made). Natural disasters are events caused by weather and other forces of nature. They are sometimes referred to as "acts of God," which implies that there was nothing anyone could have done to either cause or prevent the disaster. Examples include tornadoes, hurricanes, floods, heat waves, blizzards, earthquakes, wildfires, and **droughts**.

EDUCATIONAL VIDEO

Check out this video about how natural disasters can affect humans.

SCARY WORLD

Even a widespread infectious disease can qualify as a catastrophe if an entire community is affected.

On the other hand, anthropogenic catastrophes are ones that result directly from things people do, such as war, terrorism, and mass shootings. An industrial accident could also qualify as a human-caused disaster. For example, a massive sinkhole opened up in Bayou Corne, Louisiana, in 2012 after a salt mine collapsed. Even a riot could be considered a catastrophe if the damage got way out of control.

Whatever their cause, one thing catastrophes have in common is that they're extreme events, beyond our typical daily experiences. In fact, they can make day-to-day life impossible, at least for a

The Aral Sea was once one of the largest bodies of water in the world. A water diversion project undertaken by the Soviet Union in the 1960s led to a slow-moving catastrophe that dried up much of the sea, destroying the fishing communities that once depended on it.

time. For instance, a bad storm might result in you losing power at your house, and you may not be able to do many of the activities you normally would until the power returns. If there is a risk of flood or wildfire near your home, you may need to **evacuate**, which will involve leaving most of your stuff behind. You may not be able to go to school, and you may not see your friends until the crisis has passed.

Catastrophes often have psychological effects as well as physical ones. Child psychologists report that the psychological damage of anthropogenic disasters tends to be worse than that from natural

HUMAN-MADE NATURAL DISASTERS?

In the past, there was a clear distinction between catastrophes caused by humans and "natural" disasters like hurricanes and tornadoes. But in the future, the distinction between human-made and natural may become less clear. In 2015 a team of scientists from 20 different countries examined 28 destructive weather events from the previous year, from blizzards to heatwaves, and found that climate change played some role in half of them.

As the temperatures rise both over land and in water, weather events are expected to become both less predictable and more severe. In some regions this may mean more intense hurricanes, while in other places drought may become a regular way of life. Storms are expected to dump even more water than in the past, while the winds inside cyclones will be even more fierce. Meanwhile, rising sea levels, which are caused

SCARY WORLD

disasters. With a hurricane or tornado, nothing could have been done to stop it, and that fact is comforting to many people. On the other hand, anthropogenic catastrophes can be harder to accept, because they involve people deliberately hurting others or, in some cases, not taking action to prevent a harmful event from occurring.

FEARS OF CATASTROPHE

A lot of young kids are afraid of the dark. It's a fear that goes all the way back to our ancient ancestors, who had to be on guard against predators by melting glaciers, will mean that coastal flooding will reach farther than ever before.

Scientists believe that climate change will make disasters like this 2014 wildfire in California happen more frequently.

Current technology makes it easier for us to know about dangerous weather in advance. The National Weather Service Storm Prediction Center in Norman, Oklahoma, monitors weather and issues alerts for the entire United States.

at all times. If you can't see, you can't know whether something is creeping up to hurt you. Our imaginations get away from us, dreaming up monsters, burglars, and all sorts of threats.

Just as we can't see in the dark, we also can't look into the future. What if something terrible is lying in wait for us—not in the closet, but in the morning? We see catastrophic events on television and we can't help but think, "What if it happens to me?"

Which kind of disaster we fear depends a lot on where we are. If you are reading this book in Oklahoma, tornadoes might be on your mind. If

SCARY WORLD

you live near a coastline, you might worry about hurricanes or floods. But at the end of the day, what we all truly fear is the unknown: threats in the dark that we can't see, and events in the future that we can't predict. So what do we do about these fears?

First of all, it doesn't help to **berate** yourself for feeling anxious. Statements like "don't be silly, that bad thing will never happen" are meaningless. There's no use in denying the idea that life is uncertain, because it is. So let's begin by giving ourselves a break. Yes, catastrophes happen, and that can be scary. There is nothing wrong with a little bit of anxiety—in fact, anxiety can help you if you use it for good! This is what we'll consider in the next chapter.

RESEARCH PROJECT

Find out about a major natural disaster from the past and write a report about it. Pay particular attention to what, if anything, people did to prepare, and how they went about the recovery process. What help did they need, and who provided it?

TEXT-DEPENDENT QUESTIONS

1. Name some examples of natural catastrophes.
2. Name some examples of anthropogenic catastrophes.
3. Why might anthropogenic catastrophes be hard to recover from psychologically?

CHAPTER TWO

LIVING WITH UNCERTAINTY

Have you ever been about to go somewhere and, as you're heading out the door, somebody says, "Have a safe trip"? Or "Drive carefully"? Adults say things like that all the time, but these remarks are kind of odd if you think about it. After all, people don't have accidents because nobody told them not to! But "have a safe trip" just *feels* like the right thing to say.

Maybe it's because we understand how uncertain life can be. It's not likely that something bad will happen . . . but we have to admit that the possibility exists. None of us knows what tomorrow holds—it could be something great or something horrible. Living with uncertainty is a bargain we all make with the world.

The question is, how do we manage this? One key is to understand the difference between the words *possible* and *likely*. Think of it in terms of a visit from aliens. Is it possible that an alien ship will land in your yard? Sure, it's possible. Is it likely? Definitely not.

WORDS TO UNDERSTAND

adaptive: describes a helpful response to a particular situation.

bias: a strong prejudice; can be positive or negative.

exotic: describes something strange.

novelty: something new or unusual.

plausible: possible.

CATASTROPHES

Unfortunately, our brains love to muddy the distinction between possible and likely. Understanding how that occurs may help reduce your anxiety.

REALITY CHECK

A dangerous disease called Ebola has taken many lives, especially in West African countries such as Sierra Leone and Liberia. Ebola is not a new problem, and doctors are well aware of how to treat it. Unfortunately, countries with poor health care don't always have the resources. In those places, Ebola can rage through communities, killing as many as half the people who get it.

In 2014 there was an especially bad Ebola epidemic in West Africa. Stories about the disease were in the

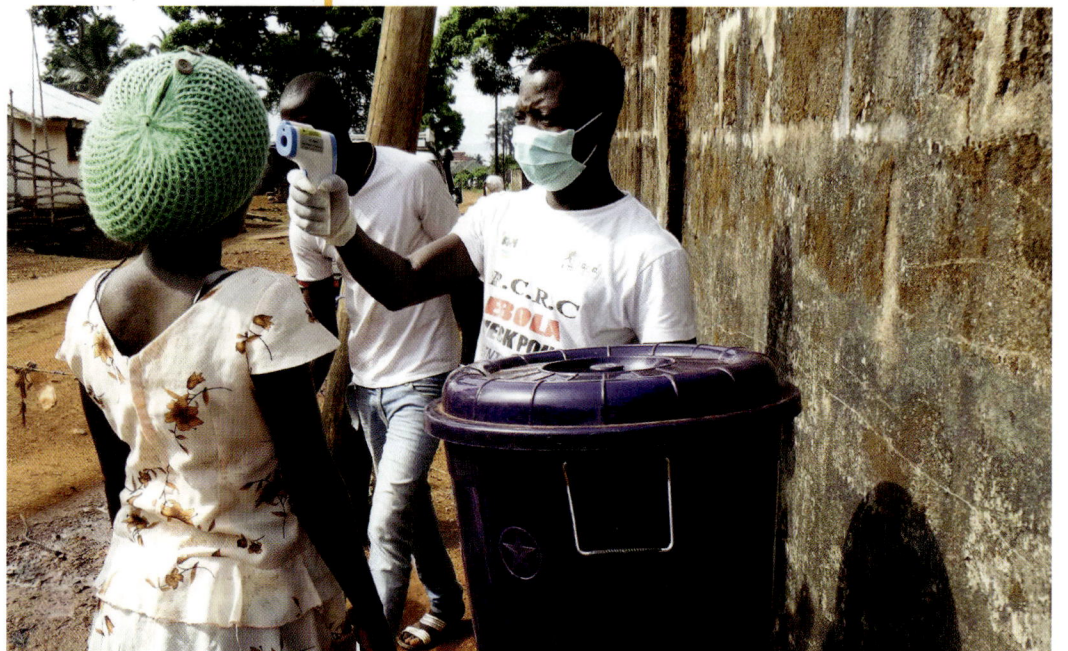

Health-care workers helped residents of Sierra Leone fight Ebola in 2014.

news every day. Many Americans were terrified that Ebola would come to their communities. And the more news people watched, the more afraid they became.

But do you know how many Americans got Ebola? Three. Two were nurses who treated the same foreign patient at a hospital, and the third was a doctor who treated Ebola patients in Africa and discovered, after he arrived home, that he had gotten the disease. All three American patients were treated and recovered just fine. But judging by the media coverage, you would have thought that Ebola was poised to spread like wildfire across the United States. Meanwhile, about a hundred people die in traffic accidents *every day*. More than a thousand Americans die of cancer *every day*. But those stories don't end up in the news.

For better or worse, we have a built-in **bias** toward drama and excitement. It might sound weird to describe something as terrible as Ebola as "exciting," but in a way it is, because it's so different from the things that happen every day. We often let ourselves get distracted by the **exotic** dangers and miss the boring ones. It's **plausible** that somebody got hit by a car because he was too busy worrying about Ebola.

Humans are bad at assessing risk because of two particular biases. First, we are naturally attracted to what some people call the "shiny object." This expression comes from a belief that a type of bird called a magpie likes to steal and collect shiny things—although animal behavior experts say this isn't even

CATASTROPHES

Every day, more than 8 million people get on airplanes and reach their destinations safely—so many that it's not considered at all newsworthy.

true! But whether you believe that magpies actually do this or not, there's no question that humans do. We love **novelty**, and this has big implications when it comes to understanding risk. As a group, we tend to overlook the somewhat boring risks that are all around us all the time, focusing instead on big, dramatic ("shiny") threats. This is why there is so much discussion about preventing terrorism but never any discussion about preventing lightning strikes, even though the latter kills far more Americans than the former.

We also have a bias in favor of stories about things that go wrong, preferring those negative stories to those about things that go well. For example, you'll never see a news story that says, "This just in: 100,000 planes landed uneventfully at airports all over the world today." You'll only hear about the few that had trouble.

LIVING WITH UNCERTAINTY

This bias is probably **adaptive**, meaning that at some point in our evolution, it was useful to us. When our ancient ancestors worried about saber-toothed tigers, they took steps to protect themselves. In that sense, worrying helped them live longer. Humans are natural problem-solvers; we like to spot things that are broken and figure out how to fix them. The down side is that we can end up constantly anxious, focused on unlikely problems while overlooking the fact that things usually work out fine.

REDUCING ANXIETY

But bad news doesn't have to make you constantly anxious. There are things you can do about it.

Let's say you live in a tornado-prone part of the country, and you often feel anxious about the idea that your house might get hit. Try to interrupt your thought process and remind yourself that your bad-news bias might be exaggerating the threat. Simply reminding yourself that you have this bias can help to keep it under control.

Also, understand that our bad-news bias makes us want to focus on some unknown future and forget about what's actually happening in the present. One concept that's getting a lot of attention these days is called *mindfulness*. Mindfulness simply means being aware of where you are *right now*. Set aside any thoughts of what you'll be doing later or of what might happen at some future point.

 EDUCATIONAL VIDEO

Check out this video about how mindfulness can help kids.

MINDFULNESS TIPS

Anxiety is a trick that your brain plays on you—anxiety wants you to focus on things that *might* happen and forget about where you are right now. But you can use mindfulness techniques to trick your brain right back. Here are some simple exercises to refocus your brain on the "here and now," rather than on the "might be."

Pause whatever you are doing and focus on your five senses. Notice something that you see right now, something that you hear, and so on. This helps you be more aware of the present moment.

Focus on your breathing. Picture air as having a particular color, and imagine the color filling your lungs as you breathe in, and making a cloud of that color as you breathe out. Do this a few times, while thinking of nothing except your breathing.

Think of something you do the same way every day, and try to do it slightly differently. For instance, if you are right-handed, then you probably brush your hair with that hand; next time, try using your left. Or maybe you always put on both socks and then both shoes; next time, put on one sock, then one shoe, and then the other sock and other shoe. Shaking up your routines can make you more aware of what you are doing. This helps you focus on the right now.

Pick up an object you use all the time—it could be something simple like your toothbrush or a complex object like a phone. Study the object carefully. Ask yourself, who made this? How did it come to be with me? How does it work? Taking the time to really notice objects we normally take for granted is another way to focus on the present.

Let's assume you're at school while you're reading these words. Is there a tornado over the school? No. Are you in any immediate danger from a tornado? No.

LIVING WITH UNCERTAINTY

Practicing mindfulness can help counteract your bad-news bias.

The second step is to get some facts. Let's continue with the tornado example: according to the National Weather Service, just over a thousand tornadoes occur in the United States every year. Depending on where you live, there might be particular times of the year when tornadoes are more likely. In the past, tornadoes were a surprise, but our sophisticated storm-tracking systems have made extreme weather events easier to predict. If you are worried, try and find out what's expected to happen. Having the facts about whatever makes you anxious can help you put your feeling of risk in the proper perspective.

And finally, find out what you can do to prepare. Taking concrete action will help quiet your anxiety because you'll know that, even if the worst happens, you'll be ready. In the next chapter, you'll read practical tips on how to be prepared rather than worried.

RESEARCH PROJECTS

Find out more about mindfulness techniques. Write down a list of techniques, both from this book and from your own research, and spend a week or two trying them out. Afterward, write down how you felt about each of the techniques. Which ones worked for you and which ones didn't?

TEXT-DEPENDENT QUESTIONS

1. What does the 2014 Ebola crisis teach us about humans and risk?
2. What biases do most people have that can increase anxiety?
3. How did those biases help our ancestors?

CHAPTER THREE

PREPARATION

Anxiety is not a fun feeling to have. But the truth is that anxiety is not 100 percent bad; it can be very useful. Whether anxiety is good or bad depends on two factors: how much anxiety you have, and what you do about it.

For instance, let's say you are feeling anxiety about a math test. If you are so anxious that you can't sleep, that's probably bad. But if worrying about the test inspires you to study, then that anxiety is actually a good thing. It motivates you to prepare for an event you knew was coming.

The trouble with catastrophes is we can't know if they are coming or not. You can end up in an argument with yourself: your rational voice says, "*it probably won't happen,*" then your anxiety whispers "*but maybe it will,*" and you go back and forth between the two thoughts. Feelings of uncertainty can cause people to spend so much time stewing about what *might* happen that they never get around to actually doing anything. In fact, one of the greatest works of English literature is a play called *Hamlet*, in which the main character spends the entire length of the play trying to decide whether to act or not.

WORDS TO UNDERSTAND

disrupt: to cause confusion or difficulty.

emergency preparedness: a set of actions someone takes in order to be ready for a possible disaster.

CATASTROPHES

Don't be Hamlet. You might be anxious, but you are not helpless. You can take small, concrete steps to prepare for whatever type of disaster you are worried about. Even small actions can go a long way toward easing your anxiety.

GET THE INFORMATION

Anxiety and uncertainty go hand-in-hand, so your first step toward reducing anxiety is to get informed. What catastrophes or disasters are a realistic concern for you? If you live in Omaha, it's probably not flooding, and if you live in Miami, it's probably not earthquakes. There's no realistic reason to fear an asteroid hitting your house . . . but a fire is something that can happen anywhere. Power outages may not sound very dramatic,

The football player Ahmad Carroll leads a kids' disaster preparedness workshop, organized by the Federal Emergency Management Agency.

PREPARATION

but they are a possibility no matter where you live, and they can really **disrupt** daily life. Ask an adult you trust to help you take a matter-of-fact look at where you live. It's important to not do this alone. If you can, get your whole family to have a conversation about which concerns are realistic and which ones aren't.

Once you have figured out what problems are worth your time, do some research. The Federal Emergency Management Agency (FEMA) has extensive information about all kinds of possible catastrophes. The U.S. Department of Homeland Security hosts a website called Ready.gov that has suggestions on how to prepare for every scenario you can think of, from chemical spills and cyber attacks to wildfires and "space weather" (www.ready.gov/prepare-for-emergencies). And finally, the American Red Cross has a Disaster and Safety Library that has checklists people can use to prepare for a wide range of potential problems (www.redcross.org/prepare/disaster-safety-library).

Much of our anxiety springs from our overactive imaginations. Instead of letting your anxious brain come up with "worst-case scenarios," seek out real-world information instead.

MAKE A PLAN

Once you have a handle on what type of emergencies to prepare for, you can set about making an emergency plan. These plans will vary depending on the type of

EDUCATIONAL VIDEO

Check out this video with emergency-preparedness tips for kids.

emergency. But speaking generally, there are a number of things you can do.

First, sit down with your family and figure out how you will get in touch with each other. Do you all have cell phones? If so, do you all have each other's numbers? Remember, though, that cell towers sometimes fail in emergencies. So how else might you get in touch if you can't get through that way? Does everybody know how to text? (Texting is often more reliable in emergencies than voice calls.) If someone in the family doesn't have a phone, how might you reach him or her?

Second, experts suggest that you then choose three meeting places: one just outside your house (such as the mailbox), one near your house (such as the street sign at the corner), and another in a different town (such as the library). Talk through a plan about how you will all get there. Here is a possible plan: "Mom will pick me up at school, Dad will get my younger brother from day care, and we will meet at Grandma's house, which is in the next town over." You can see from this example why it's important to discuss this with your family—as a kid, you can't drive or control who picks you or your brother up.

Third, make sure everyone knows how to be safe in your home (in case of a hurricane or tornado, for example), and also how to get *out* of your home safely (in case of a fire, for example). If at all possible, try to have more than one way to get out. If you live

PREPARATION

KEY NUMBERS

You probably know by now that if you are in serious danger, you can call 911 for emergency help. But there are also other numbers you should have handy just in case. Make an easy-to-read list and post it somewhere that anybody in your family can find if they need it.

The specific numbers you need may vary depending on your situation—talk to your parent or caregiver about what is most important to include. Your list should at least have:

- parent/caregiver cell phone(s);
- sibling cell phone(s);
- main phone numbers for school and work (*in case cell phones are not working*);
- friendly neighbor's contact info (*this matters because you should know how to contact someone who is physically nearby*);
- out-of-town family's or friend's contact info (*this matters because you should know how to contact someone in a different community, which might not be affected by whatever is happening where you are*).

Make sure all your important emergency numbers are stored on your phone, just in case.

in apartment building, make sure you know not just where the elevator is, but where the emergency stairs are, too.

Finally, keep a list of contact information (see sidebar on page 29), as well as any important medical information. Does someone in your family have a condition that will need attention? Make sure that all important prescriptions are written down, along with the phone number of the doctor and the local pharmacy.

BUILD A KIT

If you've got a list of phone numbers and a couple of agreed-upon meeting places, congratulations: you are already better prepared for emergencies than the average person! Getting informed, staying in touch, and thinking through a plan does not take very long, and it doesn't cost a thing. If you want to take things a step farther, though, you can—though this will require more cooperation from the adults in your life.

Many people have a physical **emergency preparedness** kit that contains materials people might need if there's trouble. How much you can buy depends on your family's finances and how much room you have to store things. But if you and your family do decide to stock an emergency kit, here are some items to consider:

- basic first-aid kit (bandages, antibiotic cream/ointment, aspirin);
- flashlights and batteries;

PREPARATION

- emergency blanket(s);
- hand sanitizer;
- multi-purpose tool ("Swiss Army" knife);
- spare chargers for electronic devices (the ones that plug into cars can be especially useful);
- tissues and sanitary products;
- extra medication for anyone with a medical condition (keep an eye out for expired medicine and replace when necessary).

Some people also store canned food and a few gallons of water per family member. (Do keep in mind, however, that you may need to rotate these supplies every year or so, depending on how they are stored.)

You may also want to add a special radio to the kit, so that you can stay informed about what's going

Not everybody has the space or the money to collect emergency food supplies, but it's a great thing to do if you're able.

PLANS FOR PETS

For many people, their family isn't just composed of humans—it also includes their dogs, cats, birds, or other pets. And in an emergency, those family members will need some attention, too.

Ideally, pet owners should be ready to take their pets with them if they have to evacuate. But this can be tricky, particularly in the case of dogs and cats, which not all shelters or hotels will accept. Make sure you give some thought to what will happen to your pets. Will a friend or family member be able to help? What about companies that board pets? Talk to your veterinarian; he or she has probably thought a lot about this issue and can give you advice about the best plan. You should also consider adding your pet's food and medication to your emergency preparedness kit.

A cat and her emergency preparedness kit. In addition to food and water, the ziplog bag contains a printout of the cat's medical information.

PREPARATION

on. Your parents' tax dollars pay for a number of sophisticated early-warning systems that many people don't even know about. The system as a whole is called the Integrated Public Alert and Warning System (IPAWS). IPAWS is also able to broadcast messages over regular and satellite radio, and on regular and satellite television—this can be nationwide, or it can be limited to local areas, depending on the emergency. Another aspect of IPAWS is an "all-hazards-warning" channel that the public can access by means of an emergency radio. These radios are sold in most department stores.

Not everybody can keep a lot of gear around, of course, and that's okay. If you've prepared the phone number list and the meeting place plan, you're well ahead of the game.

RESEARCH PROJECT

Print out the two-page emergency plan provided by the Federal Emergency Management Agency (FEMA) and fill it out with your family. It is available at www.ready.gov/sites/default/files/documents/files/Family_Emegency_Plan.pdf.

TEXT-DEPENDENT QUESTIONS

1. Name some organizations that provide solid information about disasters.

2. What are some of the phone numbers you should definitely know in case of emergency?

3. What is IPAWS?

CHAPTER FOUR

RECOVERY

This book intends to help you reduce your anxiety about whatever type of catastrophe is on your mind. Whether it's looking realistically at risk, finding out the facts, or taking concrete steps to prepare, these actions can help you feel better. That's because they help you replace a feeling of helplessness with a sense of control. But the reality is, when it comes to disasters, none of us are completely in control. Even the best advice in the world can't prevent every bad thing from happening. So if something bad does happen, it's important to remember that it's not because of anything you did or didn't do.

IMMEDIATE HELP

Humans have been coping with catastrophes for as long as we've been around. And according to United Nations data, more than 226 million people are affected by disasters every year. That means a lot of knowledge has been collected about the best ways to handle a crisis. If the bad thing comes—if the hurricane arrives, or the house catches fire, or whatever the situation might be—you and your family will have to work together to figure

WORDS TO UNDERSTAND

cognitive: having to do with how we think.

exposure: coming into contact with a thing or idea.

narratives: stories.

regress: to go back to an earlier state of being.

repercussions: effects.

resilient: able to recover from hardship.

vicarious: describing something that happened to someone else, which you can imagine.

CATASTROPHES

A Disaster Distribution Center in Griffin, Georgia, coordinates food donations to survivors of a tornado in 2011.

out what happens next. Fortunately, there are a lot of resources and help available.

The first order of business is to make sure that you and your family are in a safe location. Hopefully you have followed some of the planning instructions in the previous chapter, so you and your family know how to find one another in case of trouble. Once you are together, your parents will make a decision about the best place to go. If you need to be away from home for a while, you may stay with friends or family. Or you may evacuate to a hotel or an emergency shelter. In other situations, you may be perfectly safe waiting out the crisis in your own home.

RECOVERY

Frequently, the catastrophe itself doesn't last all that long. In other words, hurricanes usually pass by in about a day, tornadoes travel even faster, and a terrorist attack may be over in a matter of minutes. Once the immediate crisis has passed, the real work begins: recovery. Disaster recovery can include things like repairing damaged buildings and replacing broken items. But the hardest part of recovering from a catastrophe usually isn't the physical things. Buildings can be fixed, after all, and new clothes can be purchased. The hardest part of recovery tends to be emotional, or figuring out how to return to "real

RELIEF ORGANIZATIONS

Unfortunately, this book is too short to provide comprehensive information about what to do during every type of catastrophe. But here are some very good organizations that specialize in helping people in difficult circumstances. (Note that these are nationwide organizations; the best source for help may actually be a local church or police department.)

American Red Cross
www.redcross.org
1-800-HELP-NOW

Americares
www.americares.org
1-203-658-9500

FEMA/Disaster Assistance
www.disasterassistance.gov

Salvation Army
www.salvationarmyusa.org
1-800-728-7825

SAMHSA Disaster Distress Helpline
www.disasterdistress.samhsa.gov
1-800-985-5990

CATASTROPHES

life" after something really bad has happened. And, unfortunately, the recovery process sometimes involves funerals and mourning for people who were less fortunate than you were.

THE AFTERMATH

You'll go through a lot of complicated feelings in the aftermath of a disaster. You might be extremely angry at times, or incredibly sad. Although every catastrophe or trauma is slightly different, over the years, experts have identified a number of key reactions that usually (but not always) occur:

Grief. The idea that people grieve after a disaster seems like a given, but it's important to remember that we can feel grief for more than just people who've died. We might grieve over physical objects like our homes, or over particular possessions we really loved.

A young survivor of an earthquake in Muzaffarabad, Pakistan, visits what's left of his house.

Or we might experience a more metaphorical grief—for our sense of safety, or for a community that now seems changed forever.

Nagging fear. People who have been through a catastrophe are often more "jumpy" than they would be under normal circumstances. The important thing to remember about fear is that it's hardwired into us. Feelings of fear that are very strong or that last a long time can have real physical and emotional **repercussions**. It may take time for a survivor's stress response to settle down completely.

Feelings of isolation. People who have survived a traumatic event often feel somehow changed afterward. This makes them worry that they are totally unique in the world and that no one could understand how they feel. These feelings can become even more intense in situations where the survivor has to relocate. Being in a strange place without the comforts and rituals of home only reinforces the idea that the survivor is all alone in the world.

Negative judgments about one's own behavior. After a catastrophic event, survivors tend to quickly settle on their own interpretations (or **narratives**) of what happened and—importantly—on how they behaved. Frequently, these narratives are critical, and this negative self-judgment can be really harmful. For example, a young person might decide that she was a coward because she was afraid, or because she froze up and did not act at a particular moment. These judgments are totally unfair, especially where kids are concerned. But they can be hard to get over, and they can lead to constant feelings of depression, anxiety, and hopelessness.

THERAPY

People who study child psychology say that it's very normal for kids to **regress** a bit after catastrophes—meaning you might act a little "younger" than you really are. You might want more attention, support, and even cuddling than you normally would. That's totally normal, and actually it's kind of a good sign, because it means that your brain and heart are working through the terrible thing that happened. Sometimes people who've been through a traumatic experience need help with all that processing, and this is where therapy can be very useful.

One type of therapy that can be helpful for young people is called trauma-focused **cognitive**-behavioral therapy (TF-CBT). TB-CBT helps kids and teenagers make changes to both *how they think* about what happened and *what they do* in response. Developed in the 1980s, TF-CBT was originally created to help kids who had been abused by family members. Once the techniques were shown to be successful in those situations, TF-CBT began to be used to help people who survived terrorism and natural disasters.

The techniques used in TF-CBT help people replace negative narratives with more realistic ones.

EDUCATIONAL VIDEO

Check out this video about how some kids recovered from a natural disaster.

For instance, rather than constantly thinking, "I should have been more heroic," it would be healthier to think, "I did the best I could under terrible circumstances." TF-CBT also helps kids feel more comfortable about expressing negative emotions, and it shows them how to gain a better understanding of how our emotions affect our behavior. Kids practice stress-management and relaxation techniques so that they are better able to calm themselves down when upsetting things occur, such as when something random reminds them of the disaster they experienced. TF-CBT is also helpful for parents, who learn new strategies to help their kids cope with upsetting memories or emotions.

Another important concept in TF-CBT is **exposure**. But rather than using exposure to gradually conquer a phobia, TF-CBT gradually exposes survivors to the anxiety they feel about what happened to them. The very act of talking about the event helps survivors incorporate the memory of the disaster—the trauma narrative—into their lives as a whole. As time passes, the catastrophe takes its place as just one episode in the survivor's entire life, a larger narrative that has both good and bad parts.

BOUNCING BACK

What we call "normal life" is essentially a collection of rituals. You always take the same bus to the same school, you sit in the same seat with the same people around you, you come home at the same time, you eat

CATASTROPHES

HELPING OTHERS

When you hear about something terrible happening, it's natural to want to help—but as a kid, sometimes it's tough to figure out what you can do. Here are some ideas:

- Suggest to the adults in your life that you all work together on a fundraiser for people who have been hurt by the disaster.
- Start a food drive to collect donations from around your school or neighborhood. You might want to focus on "kid-friendly" foods to give to the young people who've been affected by the disaster.
- Find out if your classroom can "adopt" a classroom in the affected area. You could become class pen pals or help them restock their supplies. If you attend a church, synagogue, or mosque, find out if the kids from your place of worship could "adopt" kids from one in the affected community.
- Volunteer your time at an animal shelter that is helping pet owners in the affected area.

In New Orleans, volunteers remove debris from a house that was severely damaged during Hurricane Katrina in 2005.

RECOVERY

the same snacks, and your dad tells the same jokes. Catastrophes destroy our routines and our sense of what's normal.

This is true even if the catastrophe didn't happen directly to you. This is sometimes referred to as **vicarious** or secondary trauma. For example, if there is a mass shooting at a school and you hear about it on the news, you might feel upset even if you don't know anyone at that school. You might suddenly look at your own school differently, wondering, "Will that happen here, too?" So, in a sense, your "normal life" has been affected even though nothing bad happened to you.

It might take time for you to feel safe at your school again. That's okay. You can't expect to just "be normal" again right away, and you shouldn't be hard on yourself if you aren't. The good news is, human beings are amazingly **resilient**. Don't be afraid to ask for help if you need it. Always remember that you aren't alone. Many people have been through terrible things. And in time, you can rebuild a happy life after a catastrophe.

RESEARCH PROJECT

Research what organizations in your community will offer help during a catastrophe. This can include local government, churches, and volunteer organizations. Find out what specific services they offer, and create a booklet that gathers all their contact information in one place.

TEXT-DEPENDENT QUESTIONS

1. Roughly how many people are affected by catastrophes every year?
2. What are some ways you could help others?
3. What is TF-CBT?

FURTHER READING

American Red Cross. "Make a Plan." http://www.redcross.org/get-help/prepare-for-emergencies/be-red-cross-ready/make-a-plan.

Federal Emergency Management Agency (FEMA). "Children and Disasters." https://www.fema.gov/children-and-disasters.

Greenland, Susan Kaiser. *Mindful Games: Sharing Mindfulness and Meditation with Children, Teens, and Families*. Boulder, CO: Shambhala, 2016.

Loftis, Randy Lee. "Half of Weather Disasters Linked to Climate Change." *National Geographic*, November 5, 2015. http://news.nationalgeographic.com/2015/11/151105-climate-weather-disasters-drought-storms/.

Substance Abuse and Mental Health Services Administration (SAMHSA). "Coping with Stress during Infectious Disease Outbreaks." http://store.samhsa.gov/product/Coping-with-Stress-During-Infectious-Disease-Outbreaks/SMA14-4885.

Watts, Claire. *Natural Disasters*. New York: DK Eyewitness Books, 2006.

EDUCATIONAL VIDEOS

Chapter One: AGIeducation. "Big Idea 8: Natural Hazards Affect Humans." https://youtu.be/n73qtEojP_Y.

Chapter Two: Mindful Aotearoa. "Kids Explain Mindfulness." https://youtu.be/awo8jUxlm0c.

Chapter Three: FEMA. "Introduction to Emergency Planning." https://youtu.be/TbzvomQYJpEe.

Chapter Four: UNICEF. "Children Photograph Recovery from Disaster in Japan." https://youtu.be/2THmgK9go-U.

SERIES GLOSSARY

adaptive: a helpful response to a particular situation.

bias: a feeling against a particular thing or idea.

biofeedback: monitoring of bodily functions with the goal of learning to control those functions.

cognitive: relating to the brain and thought.

comorbid: when one illness or disorder is present alongside another one.

context: the larger situation in which an event takes place.

diagnose: to identify an illness or disorder.

exposure: having contact with something.

extrovert: a person who enjoys being with others.

harassment: picking on another person frequently and deliberately.

hypnosis: creating a state of consciousness where someone is awake but highly open to suggestion.

inhibitions: feelings that restricts what we do or say.

introvert: a person who prefers being alone.

irrational: baseless; something that's not connected to reality.

melatonin: a substance that helps the body regulate sleep.

milestone: an event that marks a stage in development.

motivating: something that makes you want to work harder.

occasional: from time to time; not often.

panic attack: sudden episode of intense, overwhelming fear.

paralyzing: something that makes you unable to move (can refer to physical movement as well as emotions).

peers: people who are roughly the same age as you.

perception: what we see and believe to be true.

persistent: continuing for a noticeable period.

phobia: extreme fear of a particular thing.

preventive: keeping something from happening.

probability: the likelihood that a particular thing will happen.

psychological: having to do with the mind and thoughts.

rational: based on a calm understanding of facts, rather than emotion.

sedative: a type of drug that slows down bodily processes, making people feel relaxed or even sleepy.

self-conscious: overly aware of yourself, to the point that it makes you awkward.

serotonin: a chemical in the brain that is important in moods.

stereotype: an oversimplified idea about a type of person that may not be true for any given individual.

stigma: a sense of shame or disgrace associated with a particular state of being.

stimulant: a group of substances that speed up bodily processes.

subconscious: thoughts and feelings you have but may not be aware of.

syndrome: a condition.

treatable: describes a medical condition that can be healed.

upheaval: a period of great change or uncertainty.

INDEX

American Red Cross   27, 37
anxiety   15, 21, 25–26, 35
Bayou Corne, LA, sinkhole   11
catastrophe
   definition of   10
    natural vs anthropogenic   10
    number of people affected by   35
    psychological effects of   12–13, 38–40, 43
   See also specific catastrophes
climate change   10, 12–13
Cold War   9
dark, fear of   13–14
Ebola epidemic (2014)   18–19
electricity, loss of   12, 26–27
emergency preparedness   27–30
    contents of kit   30–31
    for pets   32
Federal Emergency Management Agency (FEMA)   27
Hamlet   25

Homeland Security, U.S. Department of   27
Hurricane Katrina (2005)   42
hurricanes   10, 12, 13, 15, 28, 35, 37, 42
Integrated Public Alert and Warning System (IPAWS)   33
lockdowns   9
mindfulness   21, 22, 23
National Weather Service   14, 23
phone numbers   28, 29, 30, 33
relief organizations   37
risk, understanding   19–20
shootings   9, 11, 43
terrorism   11, 20, 40
tornadoes   10, 12, 13, 14, 21, 22–23, 28, 37
trauma-focused cognitive-behavioral therapy (TF-CBT)   40–41
uncertainty, living with   15, 17–18
volunteering   42

ABOUT THE ADVISOR

Anne S. Walters is Clinical Associate Professor of Psychiatry and Human Behavior at the Alpert Medical School of Brown University. She is also Chief Psychologist for Bradley Hospital. She is actively involved in teaching activities within the Clinical Psychology Training Programs of the Alpert Medical School and serves as Child Track Seminar Co-Coordinator. Dr. Walters completed her undergraduate work at Duke University, graduate school at Georgia State University, internship at UTexas Health Science Center, and postdoctoral fellowship at Brown University.

ABOUT THE AUTHOR

H. W. Poole is a writer and editor of books for young people, including the sets, *Families Today* and *Mental Illnesses and Disorders: Awareness and Understanding* (Mason Crest). She created the *Horrors of History* series (Charlesbridge) and the *Ecosystems* series (Facts On File). She has also been responsible for many critically acclaimed reference books, including *Political Handbook of the World* (CQ Press) and the *Encyclopedia of Terrorism* (SAGE). She was coauthor and editor of *The History of the Internet* (ABC-CLIO), which won the 2000 American Library Association RUSA award.

PHOTO CREDITS

Cover (clockwise): Shutterstock/Gino Santa Maria; iStock/satori13; iStock/abishome; iStock/Bluberries
Federal Emergency Management Agency: 14 Jocelyn Agostino; 26 Loaitza A. Esquilin Garcia; 32 Neily Chapman; 36 Judith Grafe
iStock: 8 Malven; 16 bauhaus1000; 20 groveb; 24 MLRamos; 29 harleebob; 31 MLRamos; 34 microgen; 42 vichinterlang
Wikimedia: 11 Arian Zwegers; 13 Marines; 18 Julia Broska; 38 U.S. Air Force/Airman 1st Class Barry Loo

Southern Lehigh Public Library
3200 Preston Lane
Center Valley, PA 18034